SCHOOL'S OUT **DAD'S** ABOUT

Barnabas
for
Children®

Barnabas for Children® is a registered word mark and the logo is a registered device mark of
The Bible Reading Fellowship.

Published by
The Bible Reading Fellowship
15 The Chambers, Vineyard
Abingdon OX14 3FE
United Kingdom
Tel: +44 (0)1865 319700
Email: enquiries@brf.org.uk
Website: www.brf.org.uk
BRF is a Registered Charity

ISBN 978 1 84101 886 7

First published 2012
10 9 8 7 6 5 4 3 2 1 0
All rights reserved

Acknowledgments
Unless otherwise stated, scripture quotations are taken from the Contemporary English
Version of the Bible published by HarperCollins Publishers, copyright © 1991, 1992, 1995
American Bible Society.

Scripture quotations taken from the Holy Bible, New International Version, copyright © 1973,
1978, 1984 by International Bible Society, are used by permission of Hodder & Stoughton
Publishers, a member of the Hachette Livre Group UK. All rights reserved. 'NIV' is a registered
trademark of International Bible Society. UK trademark number 1448790.

The paper used in the production of this publication was supplied by mills that source their
raw materials from sustainably managed forests. Soy-based inks were used in its printing and
the laminate film is biodegradable.

A catalogue record for this book is available from the British Library

Printed in Singapore by Craft Print International Ltd

SODA

SCHOOL'S OUT DAD'S ABOUT

... and other **Who Let The Dads Out?** follow-on ideas

Mark Chester

★ For Mum, Dad and Stephen ★

ACKNOWLEDGMENTS

This book, like the first in the series (Who Let The Dads Out?), is the culmination of a great deal of hard work by many people. All of those I acknowledged in Who Let The Dads Out? *have influenced this book, too. In particular I would like to thank:*

Tony, Brenda and Laura Sharp for all their support in establishing and continuing to run SODA Club.

Dirk Uitterdijk, my friend and mentor, who came up with the idea for Daddy Cool! and started it off.

Mark Lloyd for helping me to move Daddy Cool! into a new phase.

Dave Brown, the Hoole Daddy Cool! group, Dave Hollins, Ro Willoughby, Martin Ankers and Jenny Gillies for their assistance in preparing the Daddy Cool! material for publication.

Jeremy Black for helping to initiate and lead Soul Man? and for his vital contribution to the session guides in this book.

All of the volunteers who have helped with SODA Club, Daddy Cool! and Soul Man?

The Who Let The Dads Out? national leadership team. Thanks again to Tony for chairing the group in my absence.

The team at BRF for all their wise advice and enthusiastic encouragement.

It is my name on the cover of this book but, once again, all of the work that the contents represent has been shared by my very patient, understanding and precious family. Thank you, Su, Megan and Billy.

This book was written because I believe in God and I believe in his transforming love for individuals, families, communities and nations. It is an honour to serve him.

Contents

*

Introduction

As I begin to write this book, 33 miners are emerging from underground in Chile, where they have been trapped in a collapsed mine for over two months. One by one, the men rise to the surface enclosed in a specially designed rescue capsule and, when they step out of the cage, there are emotional scenes as they are reunited with their families. Wives kiss them, parents hug them and, for those who are fathers, children cling to them—happy because their fathers have at last returned home. A successful rescue has been made, men have been saved and 33 families have been liberated. But the return home of these men—these fathers—has, commentators say, not just restored families; it has also revived communities, reinvigorated a country and touched the whole world.

Watching the scenes unfold on the television made me think about how many children are waiting for their fathers to return home. For some, like the miners' children, it may be literally because their fathers are physically absent from home. Many more children are waiting for their fathers to return home in a figurative sense: that is, they are waiting for their fathers' hearts to turn towards them. These fathers may be physically present but their hearts may be elsewhere—for example, with work, with sport, with alcohol or with a social club or activity.

The first book in this series of two, *Who Let The Dads Out?* (visit www.brfonline.org.uk for details), began the process of challenging and equipping churches to reach out specifically to fathers and their children, to encourage and help fathers to 'return home' to their children. If you have read *Who Let The Dads Out?* you will know just how important I believe the relationships between fathers and their children to be. I believe that the quality of the relationships between fathers and their children has far-reaching effects; that when fathers 'return home', the impact extends way beyond the individual father–child relationship, just as the return of the Chilean miners did. You will also know that I believe all men are fathers (or should be) to all children, not only to those children they have physically conceived. The inspiration for my views comes from some simple but powerful words expressed in the very last verses of the Old Testament:

See, I will send you the prophet Elijah before that great and dreadful day of the Lord comes. He will turn the hearts of the fathers to their children, and the hearts of the children to their fathers; or else I will strike the land with a curse. (Malachi 4:5–6, NIV)

Men must 'return home' and their hearts must turn to their children if strong families and strong communities are to grow—families and communities in which faith in God is passed from generation to generation.

So, why a second book? *Who Let The Dads Out?* focused on the first stage of a strategy for churches to engage with fathers and lead them to actively consider and explore their beliefs. In this book I will introduce ideas for maintaining contact with fathers as their children grow older and for enabling fathers to delve more deeply into what it means to them to be fathers and what beliefs they hope to pass on to their children. I will describe:

- SODA (School's Out, Dad's About) Club: activity sessions for dads and children in school Reception, Year 1 and Year 2 classes.
- Daddy Cool!: a five-session parenting programme.
- Soul Man?: a format for exploring basic questions of faith and spirituality.

Before we start, though, I would like to tell you a story. Dave is a stay-at-home dad to three sons. One day a number of years ago, a friend told him about a special group for dads and toddlers at the local Baptist church. Dave was desperate to find out more: looking after three young children can be a lonely business for a man in the female-dominated world of child-rearing. He contacted our church, Hoole Baptist Church, and, after hearing about Who Let The Dads Out?, he decided to give it a go. It would be a good chance to get to know a few more dads, perhaps even some in the same position as him: a stay-at-home dad. He loved Who Let The Dads Out? from the very first session and couldn't quite believe he was seeing so many fathers in one place having fun with their toddler children. He began to look forward to it every month.

When his sons got too old for Who Let The Dads Out? he took them along to SODA (School's Out, Dad's About) Club—a similar session to Who Let The Dads Out? but for older children and their fathers.

When we offered places on a parenting programme called Daddy Cool!, specifically for dads and male carers, Dave jumped at the chance. At first he felt it was a little unusual to talk about being a dad so openly with a group of other men. 'Blokes just nod at each other in the street and that's it,' he said. 'We're not naturally expressive or open.'

But he soon relaxed. 'It was amazing. Everyone seemed interested in each other. They were just ordinary blokes and we were all in the same boat. I enjoyed having a takeaway and talking about home.'

When it came to the final session of the programme, about a child's spiritual development, Dave was again apprehensive, particularly about explaining his own beliefs. 'I was nervous about exposing my opinions but everyone gave a bit and we had learned to trust each other by that stage. I couldn't believe I was talking about these things with a group of blokes. Very, very strange.'

The experience was such a positive one for Dave that he decided to join a group for men, called Soul Man?, to explore aspects of faith and spirituality in more depth. He was in no doubt that the journey he was making through these groups for fathers had impacted his life. 'It has made me go to church more often because I think now I should give my children the opportunity to experience church. To enable them to have a choice, I need to give them a taste,' he said.

And how was it impacting on Dave's own spirituality? 'I think I definitely have a spiritual side,' he said, 'but whether there is a God or any point in praying, I don't know. It has made me realise that I need to decide what I believe—what my spiritual notions are. That's one reason why I've started the Alpha Course.'

A few years later, and Dave now goes to church with his family. He describes his beliefs as follows: 'I do have faith that things will work out. I can get anxious and worry about issues, but when I look back things have worked out for the best. I pray about family issues and concerns, and I often pray with the boys at bedtime. My faith has deepened and I get more from church than I used to.'

Dave is now a vital part of the Who Let The Dads Out? national leadership team, and I am godfather to one of his sons.

I hope that through reading and responding to this book you will discover your own Daves, because, for me, all the hard work of setting up and running these groups for fathers would still have been worth it, even if it had all been for only Dave.

*

Section 1:
I didn't plan it to be like this

Let me make a confession right at the start: I didn't plan it to be like this. It just happened. I didn't have a vision. I couldn't see where we were going. We tried all sorts of things and some things worked, others didn't. We didn't devise a strategy and plan how to implement it. We simply took the next logical step and, when we looked back, it all seemed to fit. We had a staged route for engaging with fathers and their children, getting dads to talk about fatherhood and leading them on to consider and express what they believe spiritually. So I can accept no credit for the master plan because there wasn't one—in my head, at least. I believe God had one, though, and rather than imparting it to me in one go (if he had, I fear my response would have been similar to Moses' initial reaction: 'Lord, please send someone else to do it', Exodus 4:13), he revealed his plan little by little. As a consequence, each next step we needed to take didn't seem too large or daunting. I'm glad things were in God's hands.

In a nutshell, this is what happened. We had set up Who Let The Dads Out? and it was going well—so well that we were steadily increasing the frequency of the sessions. Dirk Uitterdijk and I had run a couple of parenting programmes for dads in our church, and called them Daddy Cool! Faced with around 20 dads from outside the church coming into our building with their children every month for the Who Let The Dads Out? sessions, and having got to know some of them fairly well, we decided to offer the Daddy Cool!

programme to them as well. My friend Mark Lloyd and I led the first one. It was a success, so others followed. At first we used a published parenting programme, which was not specifically targeted at fathers. I then decided to write my own and we used that.

Whenever we ran a Daddy Cool! programme, whichever material we used, the final session was always about values and beliefs. At the end of a particular programme, a number of dads said that, despite their initial trepidation, they had enjoyed discussing their beliefs and could have gone on for longer. So in response we started Soul Man?, which was a discussion group in which men could explore aspects of faith and spirituality.

At the same time as all this was happening, some of the children at Who Let The Dads Out? were starting school and so were too old for the group. We didn't want to lose contact with these families, so my wife Su and I, with our friends Tony and Brenda Sharp, started SODA (School's Out, Dad's About) Club for fathers and children in school Reception and Years 1 and 2 classes.

The end result of this slightly uncoordinated and haphazard evolution of groups and sessions was a model for churches wanting to engage with fathers and their families, which looked like this:

Stage	Group	Purpose
Stage 1	Who Let The Dads Out? SODA Club	To engage with and build relationships with fathers and their families.

Stage 2	Daddy Cool!	To get dads thinking through and expressing what being a father means to them and what legacy they would like to leave for their children.
Stage 3	Soul Man?	To give fathers the opportunity to consider and explore what spiritual beliefs they have and what they would like to pass on to their children.
Stage 4	Whatever your church provides for those who want to know more about Christianity—for example, Alpha Course or other small group.	To teach men about Christianity and challenge them to make a commitment to follow Jesus.

I have always been slightly sceptical about 'models' that tell us how we should organise our churches or do evangelism. I am ashamed to say that I have sometimes felt a little smug satisfaction on hearing stories of a supposedly failsafe model of church that has not worked or has been discredited, and I have been delighted to discover a maverick approach to evangelism that has been highly successful. Yet here I am, presenting and advocating a model for engaging fathers.

To make me feel better, please let me justify myself. Firstly, I didn't set out to devise a model; it occurred naturally and in response to the needs of the people of our community. Secondly, I do not believe that this model is the only way or necessarily the best way for leading men to put their faith in

God. I know there are other ways. And thirdly, I recognise and would encourage you to accept that this model is simply the shell that provides support and structure to what goes on within. Without content, it is pretty worthless. I'll explain.

I was once on a walk with Su and our children, Megan and Billy. We were crossing a field and, in the distance, we could see a tree. It looked lovely, despite the fact that it had no leaves; in fact, its bareness made it more eye-catching. However, around it were similar trees, all blooming with buds and leaves. As they always do when they spot something interesting, Megan and Billy dashed ahead of us towards this tree that stood out from the rest and quickly disappeared from sight. As Su and I got closer, it became clear why the tree had no leaves, and also where Megan and Billy had vanished to. They were sitting inside its trunk. The tree was hollow: its structure looked beautiful but it would never grow again because it was empty. There was nothing going on inside—other than an imaginary tea party organised by Megan and Billy!

The same is true of the model for engaging fathers that I am offering. It is just a framework. It needs content to function. A car needs an engine, a house needs inhabitants, a tree needs something inside its trunk, and groups organised by churches for dads need substance—and I believe the substance they need is love.

In his first letter, John repeatedly emphasises the importance of genuine love in our relationships and reminds us of God's commandment to love:

We love because God loved us first. But if we say we love God and don't love each other, we are liars. We cannot see God. So how can we love God, if we don't love the people we can see? The commandment that God has given us is: 'Love God and love each other!' (1 John 4:19–21)

We need to love the fathers and their families within our communities enough to welcome them, spend time with them, get to know them and serve them. We cannot just provide an activity or a group; we must also build relationships with the people who come to it. If we don't love the fathers and children who come to Who Let The Dads Out?, SODA Club, Daddy Cool! and Soul Man? enough to build relationships with them, the model is worthless. Without love, it is simply like a hollow tree—great to have fun in but with nothing to sustain growth.

*

Section 2: School's Out, Dad's About (SODA) Club

Most of the conversations of any significance that Su and I have seem to take place last thing at night, while we are lying in bed. It is often the only time when we slow down for long enough to talk properly and make decisions. We have different roles to play in our night-time communications, which can be briefly summarised as: Su talks, I listen. Su is good at keeping her side of the bargain; I'm hopeless at mine. I have fallen asleep midway through many of our little chats and consequently missed out on crucial details of what is happening to whom, and where we are going and when. In truth, I don't like talking last thing at night; I like sleeping. However, I have to admit that some good things have come from our nocturnal discussions—one of which was the title of our group for dads and their infant school-age children.

We had decided that we needed to start to run sessions for dads and their children who had become too old for Who Let The Dads Out? and, as we got ready to go to bed one night, we began talking about what we could call the group. By the time we had each come up with several ideas, none of which seemed to fit the bill, it was nearing midnight. I had had enough and was rapidly drifting into sleep when Su shouted, 'SODA. That's it: SODA. We'll call it SODA Club.'

In my drowsy state, I had no idea what Su was driving at, nor did I really care, but I did my husbandly duty and reluctantly asked, 'Why SODA?'

'It stands for School's Out, Dad's About,' she explained.

I have to admit, it woke me up properly, because I was now beginning to feel as enthusiastic about the name as Su was. You see, it seemed the perfect title for what we wanted to create.

- **School's:** The group was for schoolchildren.
- **Out:** It was taking place on a Monday evening after school (5.30pm to 7pm).
- **Dad's About:** The children needed to bring their dads or other male carers along.
- **SODA:** The session would be like a fizzy drink, with lots of fun activities going on for the children and their fathers to do as and when they liked.
- **Club:** It would be a place where the dads and children could feel that they belonged. It would be their group.

To be honest, at gone midnight I would have agreed to anything, but, with such a great title for our new group safely chosen, I could sleep peacefully at last.

I would like to re-emphasise the point I mentioned in the introduction to this book and explored more fully in *Who Let The Dads Out?*—namely that, when I refer to fathers and dads, I am not speaking just of the men who have conceived children. In my way of thinking, which is based on the principles of community, I regard all men as the fathers of all children. We are all role models for the next generation, whether we like it or not. And so again, in this book, whenever I refer to fathers or dads, I mean the term to include all male carers and role models—that is, all men. This philosophy was captured in the strapline we used below the title 'SODA Club' in our advertising: 'For all male carers of children'.

For us, the essential characteristics of SODA Club are:

- Activity
- Competition
- Food
- Friendship

Thanks to a grant we received from our local council, we were able to go on a very enjoyable spending spree around all our local toy and games stores! The types of things we bought were:

- Sets of Geomag, K'Nex, Polly Pocket and Lego.
- Jigsaws of varying sizes and difficulty.
- Compendiums of board games, containing such games as draughts, and Snakes and Ladders.
- Table-top games such as Guess Who?, Jenga, Operation, Hungry Hippos, Frustration and Kerplunk.
- Large games (often called garden games): for example a giant Connect 4, dominoes, target mat and bean bags, giant Snakes and Ladders.
- Picture books, some of which had strong dad characters in them, such as *My Dad* by Anthony Browne. (Enter the word 'dad' into the children's book section of an online bookseller to find many more.)

The toys and games are set out on different tables around the room and are available for the dads and children to use as and when they please. We also have a simple craft activity for the families to do at each session. We charge a basic amount—for example, £2 per family—to cover the cost of the craft materials and food.

Competition

One of the most popular and controversial elements of SODA Club is indoor hockey. When we set up the club, we bought two Unihoc sets: one for adults and one for children. We also acquired two inflatable goals. It was money well spent. Many of the families have loved playing hockey. As the children have grown older, their competitiveness has begun to activate, dormant competitive streaks in the dads have re-emerged—and, boy, have they reappeared with force! It is fantastic to see a group of men and children playing team games together. Indoor hockey is a great leveller because there does not seem to be such a big difference in abilities as there might be with other sports. Most men remember to hold back a little and make space for the children to play; but, when the scores are close and the game is nearing an end, a few of us can forget to play gently, so players do need to be reminded to take it easy. Football remains popular, and different types of relay races are easy to organise and enormous fun. We have also bought a parachute; even standing and wafting it up and down in the air seems to keep the families amused, but, if you would like to do something more sophisticated with it, you can buy books containing instructions for lots of different parachute games (such as *Parachute Fun for Everyone* by Renita Boyle, Barnabas, 2011).

Food

We always incorporate food into the sessions we run for fathers, and each group has something that has become known in the culinary world as a signature dish. The signature dish at Who Let The Dads Out? is the bacon butty. The signature dish at SODA Club is toast—with real butter. The children love toast and will cover it with jam or marmalade, but the thing that gets the dads most excited is the real butter. Many are, in their own words, 'not allowed it at home', so the prospect of several slices of thick warm toast slowly absorbing pools of golden butter, accompanied by a mug of steaming tea, is enough in itself to get them out of the house on a cold, wet Monday evening.

One of the Bible stories I love tells how, after his death and resurrection, Jesus appeared, early one morning, to some of his disciples on the shores of Lake Tiberias (John 21:1–19). The disciples had spent the night fishing but had caught nothing. Jesus shouted instructions to them and, when they did as he advised, their net was 'so full of fish that they could not drag it up into the boat' (v. 6). The Bible then describes the disciples coming ashore and seeing 'some bread and a charcoal fire with fish on it' (v. 9). Jesus said, 'Come and eat!' (v. 12) and then served food to his friends. 'When Jesus and his disciples had finished eating' (v.15), Jesus and Peter got into a deep and very meaningful conversation, which led to Jesus indicating 'how Peter would die and bring honour to God' (v. 19). There are a number of things we can learn from this beautiful story about why food is so important at SODA Club and our other groups for fathers.

Firstly, the story illustrates that the eating of food has a significant place at the end of a period of work. The disciples had worked hard all through the night, and the sight of food cooking on the shore must have been a very welcome one. It offered nourishment and the opportunity to rest while eating. Similarly, given that SODA Club takes place at the end of a

21

day of work for the dads (whatever their work entails), it is fitting for food to be served.

Secondly, Jesus served the food to his disciples: 'Jesus took the bread in his hands and gave some of it to his disciples. He did the same with the fish' (v. 13). There is a powerful dynamic at work when food is served by one person to another. It provides satisfaction and fulfilment to both the giver and receiver, and it makes the receiver more willing to trust the giver and accept what else he or she has to offer. The same effect can occur at SODA Club, when the tea and toast is prepared and served to the dads, who in turn serve their children. I believe it makes the families more receptive to forming a relationship with the volunteers who lead SODA Club and helps the children and fathers to deepen their relationships with each other.

Thirdly, the story reveals that the critical conversation between Peter and Jesus, about Peter's future, began 'when Jesus and his disciples had finished eating' (v. 15). The social moments I enjoy most are those that happen after we have shared a meal with friends and remain around the table, talking. It is in these times, when we are physically nourished and feeling relaxed, that the conversation often shifts to a richer and more absorbing level—maybe from an exchange of facts to a sharing of thoughts and feelings. The same can be true at SODA Club. A conversation begun while eating toast can deepen in the moments that follow, and thoughts and feelings can be shared more openly and comfortably.

Never underestimate the power of food. There is some truth in the old saying, 'The way to a man's heart is through his stomach.' Food is truly a gift from God and we should use it well in our outreach to fathers and their children.

Friendship

SODA Club is a place to form friendships. But friendships will form and develop only when we spend time together, so it is important to try to build into your sessions the capacity simply to enjoy time together. I know this may seem like a luxury when volunteers are few and your resources are stretched to the limit, but I see it as an essential characteristic of SODA Club. In our experience, it is also more achievable at SODA Club than at Who Let The Dads Out? because fewer families attend.

For us, the places where conversations occur and friendships develop are at the door when we are greeting and welcoming the fathers and children, at the kitchen server while the families are spreading butter, jam or marmalade on their toast, at the craft table and in the 'lounge' area. I call it the 'lounge' area because we spread a piece of carpet on the floor and have two old couches and an armchair around a coffee table, which is loaded with books, newspapers and magazines. It is definitely a place for relaxing and talking.

To build in enough space during a SODA Club session for people to spend time with the families, I would recommend that you try to have five volunteers:

- A welcomer: at the door to greet people and say goodbye.
- A cook: grilling the toast and serving tea and coffee.
- A crafter: to demonstrate and help with the craft activity.
- A games leader: to organise and referee the competitive games.
- A mixer: to circulate among the fathers and make conversation.

Five volunteers is an ideal number, but we have often run sessions with fewer, and at these times it is good to ask some of the dads to take responsibility for aspects of the session. The dads often rise to the challenge willingly and enthusiastically.

SODA Club: example layout

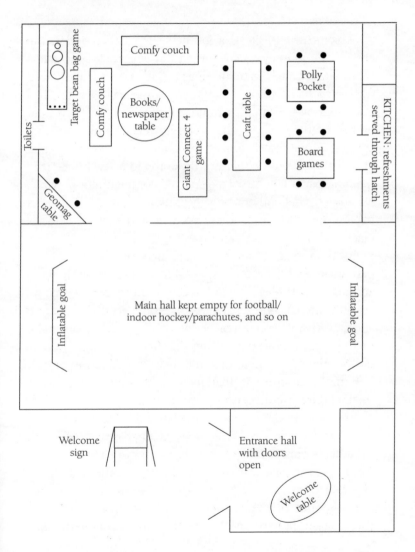

Section 3: Daddy Cool!

If, as some see it, life is a journey, then fatherhood is the part of the journey where the terrain gets rocky, the trains are disrupted and the traffic clogs up. It's difficult and, faced with the challenges of fatherhood, some will give up, bail out and look for an easier route; they won't bother trying to be good fathers. Some observers, however, think that what applies to one father applies to us all: they assume that all of us fathers would rather not make the journey. I once read the newspaper column of a respected commentator in which he argued that fathers only get involved in looking after babies 'out of kindness to our partners and because of moral blackmail'.

But then, many assumptions are made about men and, in particular, about our interests—what we like to think about and talk about. Magazine publishers seem to assume that we are only interested in sex; television producers think it's sport and advertising executives believe it's cars. They are right; men do think about these things (perhaps more than women do) but there is more to men than sex, sport and motor cars.

I think the truth is that most fathers are interested in their children and, contrary to another assumption made about men, do think about the relationships they have with their children and consider ways of improving themselves as fathers. This is not just a vague notion of mine because I am an enthusiastic father myself. It is borne out by my experience.

I was once preparing to speak to a group of men about their roles as fathers, and I wanted to find out how the dads showed their children that they loved them. The men lived in a very deprived area of a large city and all of them were unemployed. Some had addictions and others had mental health difficulties. I was talking it through with a friend and we felt that I might alienate the fathers by speaking about love. We decided that 'love' was not a word they would be comfortable with. Instead, I would ask the men how they show that they care for their children.

When I asked the men, in turn, to give examples of how they show care for their children, without exception they all talked about how they loved their children. They spoke the word 'love' without hesitation or embarrassment. Had we been speaking about their wives or partners, perhaps they would have been more coy, but when it came to their children they were happy for anyone to know how much they loved them. Another assumption set aside!

With our Who Let The Dads Out? and SODA Club sessions going well, we decided to test the theory that many dads do want to talk about being fathers, so we offered the men an opportunity to reflect on and discuss what being fathers meant for them. We had run a Daddy Cool! parenting programme with fathers from within the church and it had been a success, so we advertised a Daddy Cool! programme to the dads from the community. On our first programme, we ended up with about seven regular attenders, and the numbers attending the following programmes fluctuated between three and 13. As I mentioned earlier, at first we used material from an existing published parenting programme but, in the end, I wrote one specifically aimed at fathers and male carers—one that focused on examining the legacy we are leaving for our children. It is this programme that is reproduced in the following pages.

The Daddy Cool! parenting programme

Welcome to Daddy Cool!—the parenting programme for dads and male carers.

Why Daddy Cool!?

While most parenting programmes have mothers and fathers in mind, in reality it tends to be mainly mothers who sign up to take part. Perhaps fathers feel that talking about parenting is more the mother's domain than their own, or perhaps they would like to talk but feel a little daunted at the prospect of discussing breast-feeding with a group made up mostly of women. However, it is dangerous to assume that fathers don't want to talk about their children and their own role as parents. Given the right setting and group of people, fathers are likely to value and enjoy the opportunity to talk about parenting just as much as mothers do.

As the title suggests, this parenting programme has been designed specifically for delivery to fathers. However, not all male carers of children are their natural fathers, so the programme is equally aimed at those who fulfil the role of a father. Throughout this material, please read the terms 'father' and 'dad' to include other male carers of children.

What does the programme do?

The Daddy Cool! programme lasts for five sessions and is designed to give groups of dads the opportunity to consider and discuss the role of a father, what impact they as fathers can have on their children and what steps they can take to ensure that they leave their children a strong legacy. The programme also gives each participant the opportunity to put together a Daddy Cool! scrapbook that will capture his essence as a father and which, at the end of the programme, can be given to his children.

Who should deliver the programme?

The programme is written so that it can be picked up and delivered by anyone who has experience of or wants to try leading group discussion and activities. It is often helpful to have two people leading the programme together. Participants may respond well to a mix of styles, and it puts less pressure on the leaders than having to take responsibility for the whole of each session alone. However, if someone feels happy to lead the programme alone, it is perfectly possible for them to do so.

How do I get dads to come along?

This is the big question! Dads do generally seem more reluctant than mums to take advantage of opportunities for parenting support. By far the most effective marketing tool is personal contact, so talk to the dads at Who Let The Dads Out? and SODA Club about the programme. Give advertising flyers to these dads, and hand them out at parent-and-toddler groups, nurseries, schools and the churches in your community. Invite friends and family along, as well. Be sure to make it clear on the advertising flyers that the programme is for dads (mention, too, that this includes all male carers of children) and use 'male language'—for example:

Have you ever wished you were as cool as James Bond 007: courageous, risk-taking, a survivor and irresistible? You are—you're a dad!

So whether your children scare The Living Daylights out of you or you're The Man with the Golden Son or Daughter, this is the programme for you!

The following paragraph is an example of what you could write in a flyer to describe the programme:

The Daddy Cool! programme is all about dads helping dads, meeting together and realising that we are not alone. It is designed to give you time to think about the importance of your role as a father and what you can be doing now to ensure you leave a strong legacy for your children. It gives you a chance to consider how you can develop your children's characters, interests, values and beliefs.

Each session is designed to include a takeaway meal. The opportunity to have a takeaway with a group of men can be attractive and may make talking about being a father seem like a more comfortable prospect. Consider holding the sessions at somebody's home. A home can be less threatening than a church building, and a cosy environment may encourage the dads to relax more and take part.

How do the sessions run?

Each session is split into seven sections:

- **The goals:** The aims of the session.
- **The brief:** A short summary of the session's content.
- **The warm-up:** A choice of two activities to warm the group up. Sometimes the suggested activities are related to the session's subject and sometimes they are not. However, all the warm-up activities are intended to be fun and should be undertaken in an appropriately light-hearted way.
- **The review:** An opportunity to review the week's assignment and talk about what the participants have included in their scrapbooks. The first session includes some time to welcome people, instead of the 'review'.
- **The meaty bit:** The main section of the session, during which the week's subject is introduced and considered using a variety of methods. Activities are suggested and lists of questions to start and develop discussions are included. Handouts are incorporated.
- **The meal:** During each session, 30 minutes are set aside to have a takeaway meal together. Discussions about the session's subject can continue during the meal, but it is also an opportunity just to get to know one another a little better.
- **The assignment:** A task for the dads to do at home during the week. Each assignment is about adding something to their Daddy Cool! scrapbooks. A handout for each assignment is included.

How do I prepare?

Read through the session content, discuss it with your co-leader and decide how you will deliver the session. Think particularly about the words you will use to introduce each activity or discussion. Ensuring that the purpose of a particular activity is clearly understood by all the participants is crucial to its success.

Before the men arrive, the things you will need to think about and prepare include:

- Have you got enough seats?
- Will you make a drink for the dads when they arrive or later on?
- Where will you eat the takeaway meal?
- Have you got crockery, cutlery, drinks and glasses ready?
- When will you collect money for the takeaway meal from the dads?
- Have you got paper and pencils/pens?
- Have you got enough copies of all the handouts?
- Have you got the scrapbooks ready to give out?
- If you break into small groups, where will the groups go?

It is advisable throughout the programme to keep encouraging the dads to share what they are doing on the programme with the mothers of their children. Any fears, uncertainties or suspicions the mothers may have can then be allayed, and the dads and mums are more likely to approach parenting in a coherent way.

What should I do at the end of the session?

Take some time to reflect on how the session went. Talk it through with your co-leader. It's also a good idea to make some notes about what went well and what didn't, so that you can refer back to them when you are preparing to lead the same session again.

— SESSION 1 —

Leaving a legacy

The goals

The dads should get to:

- relax and know each other.
- understand how important fathers are to their children.
- explore the role of a father.
- decide what legacy they would like to leave for their children.

The brief

As this is the first session, it is important that the dads feel at home. The session content is focused on getting to know each other.

The dads will:

- explore the unique role of a father and what he can give to his children.
- consider the legacy each dad would like to leave for his children.
- be given an assignment to begin to produce Daddy Cool! scrapbooks as gifts to their children.

The welcome (15 minutes)

The warmth of the welcome is probably the most important part of this first session. First impressions matter! Introduce yourself and greet each dad with a handshake, then introduce the dads to one another as each arrives. Start conversations between the men so that you are free to answer the door and welcome others—for example 'John, this is Dave. He's a fireman' or 'Alan supports Liverpool. You've got a season ticket, haven't you, Alan?'

Show the men the takeaway menu and ask them to select what they want to order. It often works well to order a variety of dishes to share. Phone through the takeaway order as soon as you can.

For future weeks, use the same list (if the dads agree) and preorder the food to save time at the beginning of the session. This means you will know the exact time the food will arrive.

When everyone has arrived, introduce yourself and the Daddy Cool! programme. It is advisable to make clear right from the start that just because you are leading the programme, it does not mean you are a parenting expert. Explain that the purpose of the Daddy Cool! programme is to learn from each other by sharing experience and ideas. It is therefore important to treat each other and each other's thoughts with respect, even if we disagree with them.

Ask the dads, one by one, to introduce themselves to the rest of the group. If you feel that some of the dads may be nervous, ask them just to say their name and the names and ages of each of their children. However, if you feel it is appropriate, combine these introductions with the first warm-up below.

The warm-up (20 minutes)

Choose one of the following activities to help get to know each other and have a laugh.

Fifteen minutes of fame

Andy Warhol, the famous American artist, once said, 'In the future everybody will be world-famous for 15 minutes.' Ask the dads to explain their 15 minutes of fame, if they have already had them, or, if they haven't yet been 'famous', ask them what they hope their 15 minutes of fame will be. Explain your own 15 minutes of fame first, so that the dads have time to think.

Human sliding tiles

This is one to try only if you have sufficient space and enough people (you need at least five). Give out sheets of A4 paper and pencils, and ask each dad to write his name in large letters on a piece of paper. Lay the pieces of paper with the dads' names on them on the floor alongside each other, in a row of three and a row of two. Make the row of two up to three by adding a blank piece of paper.

Further rows can be added if you have more people, or you can make two teams and have them competing against each other, but in each grid there must always be a blank sheet of paper.

Joe	Sam	Tom
Bill	Ben	

Ask the dads to stand on a piece of paper—but not their own named piece or the blank one. Once they are in place, they must then begin working as a team to manoeuvre themselves back to their own names. They may now move on to the blank piece of paper. They can only move horizontally or vertically, not diagonally, and they cannot overtake. There can only be one person on one piece of paper at any time.

Groups do not always find this easy, so have a time limit. This warm-up helps the dads to get to know each other's names; it also helps you as the programme leader to find out a bit about the men's characters, to weigh up what roles they may take on in the group—for example leader, adviser, listener, decision maker, challenger and so on.

The meaty bit (45 minutes)

Part 1: Your unique role

This activity helps the group to consider what unique things a father can give to his children. There are no right or wrong answers!

Give out the 'Your unique role as a father' handout (see page 88 or download from www.barnabasinchurches.org.uk/extra-resources/). Split the group into pairs to discuss the statements on the handout and jot down their ideas of the unique things they can give to their children.

Come back together to share some of your thoughts and conclusions. Encourage the dads to talk about their own roles rather than just the general role of fathers. The following questions can be used to prompt and develop discussion:

- Should a father's role be the same in every family?
- What could the differences be?
- Of those we have talked about, which role is most similar to your own?
- How do your children benefit from you being this type of father?
- What is the most difficult part of your role as a father?

Part 2: Your legacy

Having considered their unique roles as fathers, encourage the dads to think of the things about themselves (their characters, values, beliefs, interests and so on) that they would most like to pass on to their children—in other words, what legacy they would like to leave.

Prepare several sets of sticky labels, with words written on each label to describe the types of legacy the dads may want to leave for their children:

Financial security	Politeness	Faith in God
Top-class education	Good profession	Deep friendships
Strong marriage	Sporting talent	Interest in a hobby
Love of animals	Support for a team	Sound parenting skills
Membership of a club	Self-confidence	Sense of right and wrong
Integrity	Honesty	Skill or craft

Leave some labels blank so that the dads can write on anything that they would like to leave for their children, which is not already covered by the labels you prepared. Provide a set of large toy bricks—for example, Duplo or a similar make—and place them in the middle of the room. Ask the dads to put their stickers on the bricks (you might now want to call them 'legacy bricks' to emphasise the point of the exercise). Then ask the dads to make a construction from the bricks.

This activity symbolises the process of building a legacy for their children. The construction should be built to show the relative importance that the dads place on each of the 'legacy bricks'. For example, the foundation of the construction might be faith in God or a strong marriage, and the heart of the construction might be a good profession or integrity. An annexe to the construction might be an interest in a hobby or support for a team.

Some men might struggle with the concept of building the construction in order to represent the legacy they want to leave for their children. If you think this might be the case, give them an alternative by saying that they can simply write down a list of the things about themselves—their characters, values, beliefs, interests and so on—that they would most like to pass on to their children.

When the dads have finished building, ask each one to explain their legacy construction—what they have included, why, and how they decided to place each 'legacy brick' (or the words they have written on their lists). Encourage the dads to ask one another questions about their constructions or lists.

When all the dads have explained their constructions or lists, you can develop a general discussion by asking the following questions:

- Who, other than you as dads, influences your children in these areas? Are those influences good or bad?
- How can you counter bad influences?
- How would you feel if your children did not follow the direction you would like them to take?
- If you had to choose only one 'legacy brick', which would it be?

The meal (30 minutes)

During this first session, the meal will need to be incorporated whenever the food arrives. It is not a good idea to let it go cold. The discussions you have started can continue while you are eating. However, the men may feel a little awkward during the first session's meal, so try to keep the conversation flowing, even if it is unrelated to the evening's subject. The most important thing is that the dads begin to communicate with each other. Future sessions may be a little easier as the dads get to know one another. When the meal has finished, continue working through the programme material from wherever you left off when the food arrived.

The assignment (10 minutes)

Explain to the dads that one of the goals of the programme is for each dad to produce a Daddy Cool! scrapbook, which can form part of the legacy he leaves for his children. Give each of the dads an empty scrapbook and explain that each week they will be given an assignment to do, to fill in part of the scrapbook. The following week, they will get the opportunity to tell the rest of the group what they have put in their scrapbook and why. It is a good idea to have enough scrapbooks that the dads with more than one child can choose whether they produce one scrapbook to be shared among their children or a scrapbook for each child.

This week's assignment is to include in the scrapbook:

- Something to represent the dad and his children together—for example, a photo, drawing or poem.
- The dad's thoughts about what unique things he can give to his children. Encourage him to discuss this with the mother of his children before recording his thoughts. His thoughts can be represented in the scrapbook through words, drawings, photos or extracts from a book—the list could be endless.
- A record of the types of legacy the father feels he would most like to leave for his children. These can be written or symbolised by a drawing (perhaps of the 'legacy brick' construction), photo, extract from a book or anything else.

For a handout on the Week 1 assignment, see page 89 or download from:
www.barnabasinchurches.org.uk/extra-resources/

— SESSION 2 —

Tuning in

The goals

The dads should get to:

- understand what tuning in to their children means.
- consider what is important to them, aside from their families.
- think about what they can do to stay tuned in to their children.

The brief

The dads should feel more at ease with each other during this session, but they may still be a little hesitant, so you should gauge the atmosphere in the group when deciding what questions to ask. Aim for the dads to go away having had a good time, even if it means you can't cover all the material.

The dads will:

- have the opportunity to review as a group the contents of their Daddy Cool! scrapbooks.
- consider what it means to tune in to their children.
- think about what passions, hobbies and interests are close to their own hearts, and what impact these things have on their children.

• be given another assignment to add to their Daddy Cool! scrapbooks.

The warm-up (20 minutes)

Choose one of the following.

Fathers on film

Ask the group to name as many television programmes and films they can think of in which a father is one of the main characters. Write down the titles of the TV programmes and films as they are called out.

You could add a competitive element by splitting the group into two teams and giving them five minutes to list as many titles as possible. Ask each team to read through their list. This may prompt some good-natured debate about whether some of the programmes or films actually have a father as a main character. The team with the longest list wins.

Ask the men to describe the characters of the fathers in the TV programmes and films. If there is time, widen the discussion by asking how they think fathers are portrayed by the media in general, or which of the fathers they identify with most.

Lounge golf

For this warm-up you will need three pieces of different coloured paper (A4 size), a golf putter, some golf balls, a carpeted floor and plenty of space.

Designate a space at one end of the room, where the players will hit the ball. At varying distances from this spot, place the three pieces of paper. Assign points to each piece: for example, two points for the closest (green), four points for the next (blue), and six points for the paper furthest away (red). The men take it in turns to hit three golf balls and score points by trying to land them on one of the pieces of paper.

It's a good idea to give the dads one or two practice shots first, so that they get a feel for the speed of your lounge carpet! If one or more of the dads finish with the same number of points, they each hit another shot to determine who goes home with the title of 'Lounge Golf Champion'.

The review (15 minutes)

Explain to the dads that this is a regular part of each session, during which they will get the opportunity to tell the group what they have put in their Daddy Cool! scrapbooks. Make it clear that all the dads can have a say, but that nobody should feel under any pressure to contribute. For some, the content of their scrapbook may be too personal to share. If possible, share something you have put in your own scrapbook to get the conversation started, and then ask whether any dad would like to tell the group how he decided what to include. Once someone has spoken, you can encourage others to do so by saying something like, 'Did anyone else decide to include anything similar?' or 'What other types of things have people put in their scrapbooks?' Encourage the dads to ask each other questions about what they have included.

The meaty bit (45 minutes)

Part 1: Tuning in to your children

The purpose of this exercise is for the group to try to reach an understanding of what tuning in to a child means.

Give out the 'Tuning in' handout (see page 91, or download from www.barnabasinchurches.org.uk/extra-resources/). Ask the group to split into pairs to discuss the statements on the handout and begin to jot down their ideas of what it means to tune in to a child.

Come back together as a whole group and ask the dads to share some of their thoughts about what it means to tune in to a child. The following questions can be used to prompt and develop discussion:

• How can you tell if a father is tuned in to his children?
• How easy is it to tune in to your children?
• How do you feel about the following statement: 'Tuning in to our children is a daily act of will. It's a decision'?
• What are the consequences if a father does not tune in to his children?

Part 2: A look at what you are tuned in to

This activity encourages the men to think about what they are tuned in to and how they balance the priorities of their commitments to their children and other things, such as work, church, social club, sport or other hobbies.

Explain to the dads that the exercise is designed to help them reflect on what is important in their lives—that is, what things they are tuned in to.

Give each man a small container, such as a bowl or jar, and several small pieces of card (just large enough to write a few words on). Ask them to write on each card one thing that is important to them in life—their passions, hobbies and interests—for example, work, golf, church, socialising, reading, watching films, cycling (one thing on each of their cards). Ask the men not to write 'family' or 'children', as you will be using the exercise to look at the things other than family and children that are important to them.

When the dads have finished writing their cards, ask them to put the cards into their containers. Each dad is now holding a representation of the priorities in their lives.

Give each man a blank piece of paper and ask him to write down a number for every one of the cards he has in his container: for example, if a dad has six cards in his container, he should list the numbers 1 to 6 on his piece of paper. Now tell the men that they must each lose one card from their container, and ask them to remove the card they would be most willing to lose—that is, the interest, hobby or whatever that they would give up if they had to lose one. Ask each man to note down, alongside the highest number on his sheet of paper, the thing written on the card he has just taken out of his container. So, if a dad has eight cards and removes one on which he has written 'Buying/selling shares' (because that is the interest/pastime he would be most willing to do without), he should write 'Buying/selling shares' against number 8 at the bottom of his piece of paper.

Repeat the process, each time asking the dads to note down what is on the card they have just removed against the next highest number on their paper, until all the men have removed all of the cards from their containers. Each dad now has a list of what he is tuned in to, in order of importance to him.

Split the men into smaller groups (of threes or fours) and give them each a copy of the 'What I am tuned in to' handout (see page 92, or download from www.barnabasinchurches. org.uk/extra-resources/). Ask them, in their groups, to talk through the implications of their lists, using the questions in the handout as a guide.

The meal (30 minutes)

You may have arranged for the meal to be delivered at a particular time so that you know how it fits into the schedule for the session. If this is the case, hold some whole-group discussion during the meal. Sometimes asking a question such as 'How did you find that exercise?' is enough to get the dads talking again. Alternatively, use the meal time to lighten the discussion and talk about something unrelated to the session's topic—for example, last night's televised football match or a current news story. Take the opportunity to ask the dads about some of the passions, hobbies and interests they have talked about during the session. You might find that some have shared interests and so will begin talking in smaller groups. This is good. The buzz of conversation during a meal is an encouraging sound and takes some of the pressure off you, as leader, to keep the discussion flowing. When the meal has finished, continue working through the programme material.

The assignment (10 minutes)

This week's assignment is to include in the scrapbook:

- A copy of the list that the dad completed in the 'What I am tuned in to' exercise. He may want to insert his children's names and the names of other significant family members at the top of his list. The Daddy Cool! scrapbook will be a gift from him to his children, so it would be affirming for the children to see that their dad has recorded them as a priority.
- Some of the dad's thoughts about his children. Sentences for him to complete are suggested in the handout, but alternative ways of recording this information can be used.
- Some information about the dad's top passion, hobby or interest (other than children or family).

For a handout on the Week 2 assignment, see page 93 or download from:
www.barnabasinchurches.org.uk/extra-resources/

— SESSION 3 —

Making memories

The goals

The dads should get to:

- think about how their own fathers have influenced the way they father their children.
- consider how they would like to be remembered by their children.
- examine how they spend their time and consider how their attitudes to spending time with their children may affect the process of making memories.

The brief

By now, the dads should feel comfortable in each other's company. However, if they don't seem to be relaxing yet, consider organising a time before the next session to get together socially—go for a drink, a curry or ten-pin bowling.

During this session the dads will:

- review what they have put in their Daddy Cool! scrapbooks.
- remember what their own fathers were like and consider what they would like their children to remember about them.

- examine how they spend their time during a typical week and what impact the time they spend with their children can have on the way they are remembered.
- be given another assignment to add information to their Daddy Cool! scrapbooks.

The warm-up (20 minutes)

Choose one of the following.

Desert Island Dads... and their guests

Tell the dads that they have each been marooned on their own desert island. Explain that they are allowed to invite three people (other than family and friends) on to their island. Ask each of the dads to say which three people he would choose—people he admires or finds interesting or entertaining, or thinks would have a useful skill for desert island life. Ask the dads to resist the temptation of choosing a person on the basis of looks alone! The people they choose might be actors or authors, comedians or musicians, characters from the Bible or fictional characters from a film, book or television programme. The dads should explain the reasons for their choices.

If there is time, you can take this warm-up a step further by telling the group that they must now all move on to the same desert island and only three guests, in total, are allowed. The dads must decide as a group which three people, of those already named, will be invited. Hold a desert island election. The dads can each vote for three people, but not their own choices. You can read out the names, ask the dads to raise their hands and count the votes, or you could hold a secret ballot by getting the dads to write their choices down on pieces of paper. The three with the most votes become the honoured guests of the Desert Island Dads.

Lounge Olympics

This consists of three throwing events: shot put, javelin and hammer. Use a ball of cotton wool for the shot put, a drinking straw (ideally a paper one) for the javelin and a short length of cotton tied around a cornflake for the hammer. Hold the shot put event first. Each dad takes a turn to throw the cotton wool 'shot put' as far as he can. The dad who throws the furthest wins the gold medal, the second furthest wins the silver medal and the third furthest the bronze. Do the same with the drinking straw 'javelin' and the cotton-and-cornflake 'hammer'. To make the Lounge Olympics even more memorable, you could make some simple medals with ribbons and discs of different coloured card, and award them to the winning dads.

The review (15 minutes)

This is a regular part of each session during which the dads get the opportunity to tell the group what they have put in their Daddy Cool! scrapbooks since the last session. Remind the dads that they can all have a say but that nobody should feel under any pressure to contribute. Some may prefer to keep the content of their scrapbooks private. Ask whether any dad would like to share with the group how he decided what to include in his scrapbook. Once someone has shared, you can encourage others to do so by saying something like,

'Did anyone else decide to include anything similar?' or 'What other types of things have people put in their scrapbooks?' Encourage the dads to ask each other questions about what they have included.

The meaty bit (45 minutes)

Part 1: Memories of your father

Tell the dads that the next part of the session will give them the opportunity to explore their memories of their own fathers. Explain that this exercise is based on the idea that our approach to family life, and consequently how we parent our children, is often influenced by the way we have been parented ourselves.

Be aware that, for some dads, reflecting on how they have been fathered may be extremely painful. Acknowledge to everyone that this may be the case, and stress that people can participate as much or as little as is comfortable. Emphasise, also, that whatever is discussed must remain confidential. A dad may be recently bereaved, or his father may have been absent or violent or showed favouritism. If you suspect this, warn the whole group at the previous session so that they can come mentally and emotionally prepared.

Give out the 'Memories of my father' handout (see page 95 or download from www.barnabasinchurches.org.uk/extra-resources). Split the group into threes to discuss the father-type descriptions on the handout and to consider which most accurately portray their own fathers.

Come back together as a whole group and ask the dads to share (they may need a few minutes to think before answering):

- what they would most like their children to remember about them.
- what they feel they must do now to ensure that those memories are made.

Part 2: Using your time to make memories

This exercise helps the group to examine how they spend their time, what their attitudes to spending time with their children are, and how those attitudes may help or hinder the process of creating good memories.

Explain that the exercise will help the dads to look at how they spend the hours over the course of a typical week. Prepare a chart to represent a week (one for each man), laid out as follows:

	Sleep	Work	Meals	Chores	Hobbies	Children	Other
Monday							
Tuesday							
Wednesday							
Thursday							
Friday							
Saturday							
Sunday							
TOTAL							

Ask the dads to estimate for each day how their time is apportioned across the categories and record the hours in the table. For example, a typical Monday for one of the dads may look like:

	Sleep	Work	Meals	Chores	Hobbies	Children	Other
Monday	8 hrs	9 hrs	2 hrs	1 hr	1 hr	2 hrs	1 hr

Then ask the dads to total the figures in each column so that each dad now has an illustration of how he spends the hours in a typical week.

Give out the 'Time and memories survey' handout (see page 98, or download from www.barnabasinchurches.org. uk/extra-resources/). Split the men into small groups and ask them to complete the survey in the handout and discuss their responses.

Come back together as a whole group and ask the dads to share some of their thoughts about the survey they have just completed and discussed. Lead the conversation on to discuss how different we may be from the people around us if we are going to make time for our children. Does that create problems for anyone in the group?

The meal (30 minutes)

By this third session, the dads may, without prompting, be talking to each other in smaller groups of twos and threes while they eat their meal. Sit back, relax and enjoy the conversation yourself. When the meal has finished, continue working through the programme material.

The assignment (10 minutes)

This week's assignment is to include in the scrapbook:

- a record of the memories the dad has of his own father.
- the dad's thoughts on how he would like to be remembered by his own children.
- something to show what the dad most likes to do with his children.

For a handout on the Week 3 assignment, see page 100 or download from:
www.barnabasinchurches.org.uk/extra-resources/

— SESSION 4 —

Inspiring respect

The goals

The dads should get to:

- consider what will make their children respect them.
- identify which respect-inspiring characteristics they already have and which ones they need to work on.
- think about how well they listen to their children and what effect their listening may have.

The brief

This is the second-to-last session, so start talking with the dads about what you could do when the programme has finished. Something that often works well and appropriately marks the end of a programme is for the group of dads to take their children on a day trip—for example, a trip to the seaside on the train. It also gives mums a bit of time off, which they often appreciate! Consider continuing to meet as a group, perhaps on a monthly basis. Are there any follow-on programmes that the dads could be invited to take part in? Could you invite other fathers to join the group?

During this session, the dads will:

- review what they have put in their Daddy Cool! scrapbooks since the last session.
- consider what characteristics they respect in other people.
- reflect on how strong those characteristics are in themselves.
- take part in an exercise to increase their awareness of how their children might feel when their dads don't listen to them, and to consider the impact of good listening and sometimes saying 'sorry'.
- be given another assignment to add more information to their Daddy Cool! scrapbooks.

The warm-up (20 minutes)

Choose one of the following.

Gentlemen of the press

Ask each dad to think of two incidents in his life—his proudest moment and his most embarrassing moment. Give out pieces of paper and pens and ask the dads to write a newspaper headline for each of these two moments. Give a few examples to help them think creatively:

- Baby-Face Dad. Visitors Say Newborn Daughter is Image of Her Father
- Turkish Delight as Couple Tie the Knot in Istanbul
- Stupid Cupid's Arrow Misses its Mark: Man Forgets Valentine's Day
- Sugar Daddy! Man Feeds Baby Son Chocolate at One Day Old

Ask the dads to read out their headlines and explain the stories behind them.

Blowpipe ping-pong

The object of this game is for the dads to compete against each other at manoeuvring a ping-pong ball around a series of obstacles by blowing it with a drinking straw. The winner is the person who navigates the obstacles in the fastest time. You will need a ping-pong ball, several drinking straws and items for obstacles, such as bottle tops, pebbles and yoghurt pots.

Give each dad a drinking straw. Set out four obstacles in a row on the floor and get the first dad to take his place at the starting point with his straw and the ball. Shout 'Go' and get all the other dads to count out loud as the first dad blows at the ball through his straw to manoeuvre it around the obstacle course. The dads should stop counting when the ball passes the last obstacle. Each dad takes it in turn to do the course, and the winner is the person who takes the least time. You may need to help regulate the speed of the counting to make it fair! Alternatively, use a stopwatch.

The review (15 minutes)

Invite the dads to share what they have put in their Daddy Cool! scrapbooks since the last session. Encourage them to ask each other questions about what they have included.

The meaty bit (45 minutes)

Part 1: What is respect?

Explain to the group that this session is about inspiring respect. Ask for a few definitions of what we mean by 'respect'. Explain that the aim of the next part of the session is to decide what respect is, and to consider the things we do as fathers that may gain respect from our children and the things we do that may cause our children to disrespect us.

Give out the 'Elements of respect' handout (see page 102, or download from www.barnabasinchurches.org.uk/extra-resources/). Ask the group to work in pairs to decide what they think are the three characteristics most likely to encourage children to respect their fathers.

Come back together as a whole group and ask each of the pairs to share their three characteristics with the rest of the group. Write down the suggestions so that all the dads can see them.

Give out the 'Self-audit of respect' handout (see page 103, or download from www.barnabasinchurches.org.uk/extra-resources/). Ask the dads to write into the table the list of characteristics suggested by the whole group, and then score themselves against each one. This should help the men to think through their strengths and weaknesses. Stress to the dads that the exercise is not meant to make them feel guilty, but just to increase their awareness of their own characteristics and how they might be viewed by their children.

Come back together as a whole group and, if you think the men would be open to do so, ask them to share what conclusions they have reached about their own characteristics. Alternatively, ask the dads to take away their 'Self-audit of respect' and be pleased about the things they are good at, as well as thinking about ways in which they might develop more 'respect-inspiring' characteristics.

Part 2: Practising respect

One of the hardest 'respect-inspiring' characteristics to master is being a good listener to our children.

This exercise is designed to help the dads experience what their children may feel when faced with a non-listening parent. You will split the dads into pairs; one dad will talk to the other for two minutes about work or a hobby. The listening dad actively listens for the first minute but then loses interest and begins to show signs of not listening. The talking dad will not be expecting this and so will experience a little of what children may feel when their fathers don't listen to them.

To introduce this exercise, it is best to say only that the dads are going to take part in an exercise about respect and that they must follow the instructions they are given. Split the dads into pairs and give out the talking/listening briefs. For each of the pairs of dads, give one dad a 'talking' brief and the other dad a 'listening' brief (see page 104, or download from www.barnabasinchurches.org.uk/extra-resources/).

Tell the whole group that you will let them know when there is only a minute to go, and then again when the exercise is complete. Ask the dads to start talking. After a minute, indicate the time left by, for example, shouting 'Minute to go' or blowing a whistle. At the end of the second minute, call an end to the exercise and bring the dads back together.

If they have not already realised, explain to the 'talkers' what the 'listeners' had been asked to do. Ask the 'talkers' to explain how they felt when the 'listeners' stopped listening. After a few people have shared how they felt, ask how the exercise might help us understand the way our children feel when we fail to give them our full attention. Use the following questions to develop the discussion further:

- How well do you listen to your children?
- Why is it so difficult to listen?
- How does it make you feel when someone really listens to you?
- As fathers, we all make mistakes. When you fail to listen to your children, would you ever say sorry?
- When you say sorry to your children, will they see it as a strength or a weakness?

The meal (30 minutes)

By now, the dads should quite naturally chat with one another, so let the conversation flow and, when the meal has finished, continue working through the programme material.

The assignment (10 minutes)

This week's assignment is to include in the Daddy Cool! scrapbook:

- a record of whom the dad respects and why.
- the dad's thoughts about the characteristics he sees in his children that he thinks will, in time, make them good fathers/mothers/role models for their own children.

- something to show what the dad likes to hear his children talk about.

For a handout on the Week 4 assignment, see page 105 or download from:
www.barnabasinchurches.org.uk/extra-resources/

Nurturing values and spiritual beliefs

The goals

The dads should get:

- to share their values and beliefs with each other.
- to identify what practices are good for passing on values and beliefs.
- to record their values and beliefs for their children.
- to write final messages to their children in their Daddy Cool! scrapbooks.

The brief

As this is the last session of the programme, the suggested structure is slightly different. The assignment is incorporated into the session's activities so that, by the end of the session, the dads' scrapbooks will be complete. The meal is moved to the end of the session so that, in the informal atmosphere at the end of the meal, certificates/gifts can be given out to mark the dads' involvement in the programme and plans can be made for follow-on activities.

During this session the dads will:

- get the opportunity to say what their own values and beliefs are, and what values and beliefs they hope their children will grow up with.
- take part in an exercise to identify the positive things they can do to pass on their values and beliefs, as well as the things they should avoid doing.
- finish off their Daddy Cool! scrapbooks.
- be presented with certificates/gifts.
- discuss plans for follow-on activities.

The warm-up (20 minutes)

Choose one of the following.

'Who said that?'

Read out the following well-known quotes and ask the dads to write down who said them. Get the dads to swap papers and mark the answers as you read them out.

'It's not easy to juggle a pregnant wife and a troubled child, but somehow I manage to fit in eight hours of TV a day.' (Homer Simpson)

'Life is like a box of chocolates… You never know what you're gonna get.' (Forrest Gump)

'When I was a boy of 14, my father was so ignorant I could hardly stand to have the old man around. But when I got to be 21, I was astonished at how much he had learned in seven years.' (Mark Twain)

'Float like a butterfly, sting like a bee.' (Muhammad Ali)

'This is my Son, whom I love; with him I am well pleased.' (God)

'I cannot forecast to you the action of Russia. It is a riddle wrapped in a mystery inside an enigma.' (Winston Churchill)

'And so, my fellow Americans: ask not what your country can do for you—ask what you can do for your country.' (John F. Kennedy)

'It is a wise father that knows his own child.' (William Shakespeare)

'Some people think football is a matter of life and death… I can assure them it is much more serious than that.' (Bill Shankly)

'I have a dream.' (Martin Luther King)

Find the missing cards

Take two packs of playing cards and remove five cards from each pack. Keeping the packs separate, shuffle the remaining cards. Split the group into two teams and give each team one of the packs of playing cards. The teams must compete against each other to find out which of the cards from their packs are missing. The winner is the first group to correctly establish their missing cards.

The review (15 minutes)

Invite the dads to share what they have put in their Daddy Cool! scrapbooks since the last session. Encourage them to ask each other questions about what they have included.

The meaty bit (30 minutes)

A little less time is spent on 'The meaty bit' this session to allow more time for the meal and certificate/gift-giving and to enable the final assignment to be incorporated into the session's activities.

Part 1: My values and beliefs

It is useful to start the main part of the session by finding out what the men's own values and beliefs are and what they hope for their children. Ask the dads to take turns to describe their own values and spiritual beliefs. If you know there are people within the group who are likely to have different values or beliefs from the rest, be sure to acknowledge that there will be differences in what people say and that each person's views will be respected. It is also a good idea to say that if anyone does not want to explain their values and beliefs (sometimes these things are very personal), they can pass. Start the process by explaining your own values and spiritual beliefs and what you hope for your children, so that others have time to think about what they will say.

Part 2: How we pass on values and beliefs

Explain to the dads that they are now going to look at the way values and beliefs are passed on from parents to children, by reading the case studies of three families. Split the men into groups of about three. Ask them to read through the case studies in the 'Values and beliefs case study' handout (see page 107, or download from www.barnabasinchurches.org.uk/extra-resources) and identify what they think each set of parents is doing that is good for passing on their values and beliefs, and what is bad. After giving the groups enough time, come back together and prompt some whole-group discussion by asking:

- Having looked through the case studies what do you think we, as fathers, need to do to pass on our values and beliefs?
- What do we need to avoid doing?

The assignment (15 minutes)

Rather than giving the dads any 'homework' after the final session, this week's assignment to add something to their Daddy Cool! scrapbooks can be incorporated into the session's activities. The assignment is to include:

- a record of their own values and beliefs;
- what values and beliefs they hope their children will have, and why
- a final statement/message to their children.

For a handout on the Week 5 assignment, see page 110 or download from:
www.barnabasinchurches.org.uk/extra-resources/

The meal (40 minutes)

As this session is the last one of the programme, you might want to arrange for the food to be delivered a little later so that the session finishes with the meal. It is good to take some time at the end of the session to mark the completion of the programme, and straight after the meal is often an ideal opportunity. Thank the dads for taking part and give them each a simple certificate to mark their involvement in the programme. You can suggest that they might want to put the certificates in their scrapbooks. If finances permit, it is also a lovely gesture to give each of the men a gift—perhaps a book about fatherhood. You could print off a short message on a sticker, and put it on the inside cover of the book. Write something like:

Tony,
   Thanks for taking part in Daddy Cool! It's been great having you involved.
   Mark (on behalf of Hoole Baptist Church)
   Spring 2011

You might also want to use this time to make the final arrangements for any follow-on activities you are planning, such as a day-trip, a men's games evening or another programme. If the dads have enjoyed the final session, they might want to meet again to explore values and beliefs in more depth. Consider setting up a Soul Man? group, described in the next section of this book.

Section 4: Soul Man?

The Daddy Cool! programme I was leading had gone well and we were approaching the final session. I was a little anxious because I wondered how freely the group of men would express their values and beliefs; I was concerned that they might be nervous doing so. I started the session by explaining, as succinctly as possible, the essence of my own faith. My co-leader explained his conviction (he was an atheist) and we then invited the other men to describe their beliefs. The ice was quickly broken as it became clear that there were various ideologies being expressed and that it was an environment in which all thoughts and notions would be welcomed. The conversation flowed as we all relaxed.

A week or so after the session, one of the dads who had taken part confessed to me that he had almost not come. In the days leading up to it, he had become increasingly nervous about discussing values and spiritual beliefs in a room full of men. It was not something he had ever done. He'd felt he might be embarrassed and that his views might isolate him from the rest of the group. He told me that he had been wrong: he had thoroughly enjoyed the evening and was glad he had not pulled out. In fact, he said that, in his opinion, it was the best session of the programme.

Another dad spoke to me and expressed similar sentiments about the session. He said that he had never publicly stated his beliefs and had found it startling and refreshing to have such an open discussion among a group of his friends. I realised that there was an unrecognised appetite and unacknowledged need within some men to consider their own spirituality, to ask themselves some basic questions about whether there is a God and, if so, what implications it had for them and their children. I decided I needed to respond to this and give dads an opportunity to take the discussions further and deeper, so we started a monthly group called Soul Man? It delighted me that one of the participants from Daddy Cool!, Jeremy Black, joined with me to develop the Soul Man? format and prepare and lead sessions.

Let me start by telling you what Soul Man? is not:

- It is not a course with a set number of sessions and a programme to be worked through.
- It is not a debating society in which the participants attempt to win or lose arguments.
- It is not a tutorial group in which one person teaches the rest.

Soul Man? is:

- a discussion group in which the participants are encouraged to express their thoughts and beliefs, whatever they may be.
- a place to question one another—not to persuade or convince but to try to understand what each person thinks.
- an environment in which it is safe to re-evaluate and develop one's thinking about spiritual matters.

Two things might concern you about this format. Firstly, how do we encourage the men to explore the Christian faith specifically, and what it means to follow Jesus? For me, the answer rests with the Christians who are in the group: through their personal testimony about their faith, their relationships with the other men and their prayers for those who have not yet committed to following Christ, they may be the catalyst for opening their friends' hearts and minds to God. If, through Soul Man?, one of the dads decides he would like to explore the Christian faith in more depth, it is clearly important for your church to provide that opportunity through whatever programme you offer to people who are curious about Christianity. But the aim of Soul Man? is to take men from a position in which they have never thought through or spoken about spiritual beliefs to a place in which they begin to consider and express their own spirituality. We hope it will be a small but significant step in the process that ultimately leads the men to find God and accept his authority in their lives.

Your second concern could be that the Soul Man? format sounds like a bit of a free-for-all. It is not intended to be, and, in fact, I believe it will be far less fulfilling for the participants if it develops into a format in which the only leader is the discussion itself. Someone does need to take responsibility for providing a structure, facilitating the discussion and keeping things on track, otherwise it can wander aimlessly.

In my opinion, the most important ability you need, to lead a Soul Man? group successfully, is the ability to ask questions. If someone asked me what the essence of a Soul Man? session is, my answer would be simply 'Questions'. It is all about asking ourselves and others questions—and you must set the standard as the leader of the group. So often, we seek to share our faith with others by telling them what we believe, when a better way to start would be by asking them what they believe. Asking questions leads to self-discovery. For example, 'What do you believe?' makes us begin to formulate an answer about something we may have never addressed before. I have sometimes been asked, 'What do you think?' and have been surprised by my own words as I've been answering. Verbalising helps us to clarify our thoughts and beliefs.

If we look at the example of Jesus' life, we can see just how powerful the use of questions can be. He used them in some surprising situations. One day, Jesus was teaching in the temple when the chief priests, the teachers and the nation's leaders put a question to him. 'What right do you have to do these things? Who gave you this authority?' they asked (Luke 20:2). If we put ourselves in Jesus' shoes, a natural response in such a situation would be for us to use the opportunity presented by such questions to give a direct answer: we might explain that we serve God and try to convince the questioners that our authority comes from him. Jesus, however, does something completely different. He responds with questions of his own: 'Who gave John the right to baptise? Was it God in heaven or merely some human being?' (v. 4).

After deliberating over their answer, and considering the implications of what they might say, the priests, teachers and leaders say, 'We don't know who gave John the right to baptise' (v. 7). Jesus then draws the conversation to a close by saying, 'Then I won't tell you who gave me the right to do what I do' (v. 8).

By asking questions, Jesus defused a situation and avoided setting himself up for public criticism. He also made the questioners think through and evaluate (albeit for their own protection) the possible answers to their own questions.

Later in Luke 20, Jesus does it again. Some of his enemies say, 'Tell us, should we pay taxes to the Emperor or not?' (v. 22). Once more, Jesus resists the obvious temptation to answer the question directly. Instead, he gets them to show him a coin and asks a question himself: 'Whose picture and name are on it?' (v. 24). The people respond that it is the Emperor's picture and name, and Jesus concludes the matter by saying, 'Give the Emperor what belongs to him and give God what belongs to God' (v. 25). Jesus' enemies 'were amazed at his answer and kept quiet' (v. 26). Jesus has skilfully used a question to lead people to their own conclusions.

Questions, then, are crucial to a Soul Man? group, and it is wise to prepare in advance. Over the next pages, I have set out six possible themes for Soul Man? sessions (these are themes that Jeremy and I have used), some questions to use in guiding the conversation, and suggestions for activities on which to base those questions. These suggestions are only a guide; you may want to devise your own themes, activities and questions. In fact, I would encourage you to consult the members of your Soul Man? group about what subjects they want to consider. It's a good idea to plan the themes of the meetings in blocks—say, three or four months at a time—so that, wherever possible, there is a coherent flow through the sessions.

None of our projects for fathers would be complete without food, and, as with Daddy Cool!, Soul Man? sessions always include a takeaway meal, the cost of which is shared between the participants. The conversation continues and often deepens as the meal is eaten.

— THEME 1 —

The soul

Does the soul exist? What is a soul? What is the soul's function?

Ice-breaker question

Which room in your house would you say has a 'soul', and why?

Activities

- Circle the words that best describe a soul:

  Essence   Core   Hindrance   Conscience   Nature

  Personality   Navigator   Identity   Will   Thoughts

  Feelings   Imagination   Barrier   Life   Guide

- List the main functions of the soul.
- Describe the effects if a person were to lose his/her soul.

Discussion questions

- Do you think you have a soul?
- Where do you think your soul comes from?

- Are you a soul with a body, or a body with a soul?
- Is a soul purely good or can it be bad?
- Does a soul change/develop/begin/end?
- How do you keep a soul fit and healthy?
- What happens to a soul if it is not looked after?
- Where does a soul go when a person dies?
- How do we enable our children to understand and look after their souls?

— THEME 2 —

God

Does God exist? How do my beliefs about God affect my life?

Ice-breaker question

Which person—living or dead, famous or not—would make a good god? Why?

Activities

- Draw a symbol to represent your thoughts about God.
- If you don't believe in God, imagine someone convinced you that God does exist and write down three changes it would make to the way you live your life.
- If you do believe in God, imagine someone convinced you that God does not exist and write down three changes it would make to the way you live your life.

Discussion questions

- Why do you believe in God?
- Why don't you believe in God?
- How do your beliefs about God affect the way you live your life?

- What does your belief/disbelief in God demand from you?
- What does your belief/disbelief in God offer to you?
- What are the risks of not believing in God?
- What are the risks of believing in God?
- Is it generally good for society that people believe in God, or generally bad? Why?
- What would you like your children to believe about God?
- How do you encourage that belief?

— THEME 3 —

Prayer

What is prayer? Is prayer worthwhile?

Ice-breaker question

What was the best present you ever asked for and received? What present have you asked for and were disappointed not to receive?

Activities

- If you came across a picture entitled 'Prayer', what would you would expect to see in the frame? Draw it on a sheet of paper.
- Choose one of the following words, which you feel best describes prayer:

    Insurance   Hope   Expression   Responsibility
            Conversation   Appeal

- Describe a situation in which you prayed and your prayers were answered or not answered.

Discussion questions

- Where does the instinct to pray come from? Is it natural or unnatural?
- Are those who don't pray suppressing their instinct?
- People of little or no faith often resort to prayer in difficult circumstances. Why?
- Why do people feel so disillusioned when they think their prayers have not been answered? Why do they still pray again?
- Do you pray? What categories would most of your prayers fall into?
  * Giving thanks
  * Asking for something for yourself
  * Asking for something for others
  * Confession of wrongdoing
  * Expression of anger or disappointment with God
  * No prayer at all
- Who do you pray to? What situations do you pray in? Where do you pray? How do you pray?
- Do you want to encourage your children to pray? If so, how could you do this?

— THEME 4 —

Right and wrong

Do right and wrong exist? How do we decide what is right and what is wrong?

Ice-breaker question

If you had the power to establish a new law for people to follow, what would it be?

Activities

- The traditional seven deadly sins are pride, envy, gluttony, lust, anger, greed and sloth. Compile a list of seven modern sins to replace them. You may keep any that you think are still valid.
- If you had to choose the seven most important modern virtues, what would they be? Compile a list alongside the seven modern sins.
- Write definitions of 'right' and 'wrong'.

Discussion questions

- Do you believe in the concepts of right and wrong?
- Where have our notions of right and wrong come from?

- Are there any absolutes? If so, who decides?
- Can we believe in right and wrong without a religious belief?
- Is it acceptable for us to have different views about what is right and wrong?
- How do we function as a society if we cannot agree what is right and wrong?
- Which is most important when judging whether something is right or wrong: the intentions, the actions or the consequences?
- What are the consequences of doing right?
- What are the consequences of doing wrong?
- Are some wrongs worse than others?
- Are some rights better than others?
- Do we need to teach our children a sense of right and wrong, or do they develop it instinctively?
- What do we need to do to pass on our values to our children?

— THEME 5 —

Life after death

Is there life after death? Will my actions in this life affect my life after death?

Ice-breaker question

If you were appointed the gatekeeper of heaven, what criteria would people have to fulfil before you allowed them in?

Activities

- Come up with one word to describe your attitude to the concept of life after death.
- List the three core characteristics that life after death would have to possess to make it appealing to you.
- Write down the differences in the way you would live your life on earth if you knew (a) that life after death did exist, and (b) that life after death did not exist.

Discussion questions

- Do you believe in life after death?
- If there is no life after death, what is the point of life on earth?

- What might life after death be like?
- What might determine who receives life after death? Who decides?
- If there is life after death, will everyone receive it, or only be certain people?
- Do we earn our life after death? If so, how?
- Might there be different types of life after death? What would they depend upon?
- What form will we take, if there is life after death?
- If there is life after death, will we recognise people from earth? Will we be reunited with our family and friends?
- Should we talk about life after death with our children? Should we introduce the subject to them or should we wait for them to raise it?
- At what age are children ready to think about life after death?

— THEME 6 —

Church

What is the point of church? Is church relevant to me?

Ice-breaker question

What is your favourite day of the week, and why?

Activities

- Explain why you go to church: is it out of a sense of duty or guilt, because it is a tradition, to socialise, to please another family member, or to worship God with like-minded people?
- Explain why you don't go to church: is it because you never have, you don't believe in God so it has no relevance, you do believe in God but you seek to express your faith aside from church, you have had a bad experience at church, or you would rather do other things with your time?
- Describe any experiences you have had of going to church.
- List the ways in which you think churches contribute to modern-day life.

Discussion questions

- What do you think a church is/should be?
- Is church about Sunday mornings, buildings or people?
- Overall, is church a positive institution or a negative one?
- What would the world be like if church did not exist? Would it be better or worse?
- Is becoming a member of a church an essential part of having a spiritual belief?
- Is church really about giving or about taking?
- Do you think a church is/should be essentially different from other clubs (for example, a health club or book club)?
- Could you ever see yourself joining a church? What would encourage you to do so? What would deter you?
- What would you like your child's attitude to church to be? What do you need to do to encourage this attitude?

*

Section 5: Final words

I hope that many of the fathers in your community find their way along to one of your Who Let The Dads Out? or SODA Club sessions. I hope they progress from there on to your Daddy Cool! programme and then into your Soul Man? group. I hope they end up on your Alpha course or whatever other provision your church makes for those who wish to explore Christianity. But, ultimately, I hope that the fathers and their families discover God. I hope that they begin to believe in him, trust him and follow him. For some, this could happen quickly; for many others, it will be a slow process. For example, it could take many years from your first contact with a father at a Who Let The Dads Out? session before he even chooses to join your Soul Man? group. I would therefore encourage you to discuss a strategy for engaging with fathers and their families, with the leaders and members of your church. Talk about it, pray about it and, as one body of people, commit to it wholeheartedly for the long term.

You won't reach every father in your community, and not all those you do reach will end up devoting their lives to following God. But I am certain you will make a difference in the lives of many families—that you will help to turn the hearts of fathers to their children, and the hearts of children to their fathers, and that you will help to turn the hearts of some fathers to their own Father in heaven. In the work that you do—with God's grace, Jesus' teaching and the power of the Holy Spirit—you can change the course of families and affect many generations to come. God bless you as you do so.

Handouts and session assignments

*

Your unique role as a father

Discuss the following statements and jot down whether you agree or disagree with them. As you do so, write down any thoughts about what unique things you as a father can give to the children in your family:

- Mums are better than dads at the practical aspects of looking after children.

- A dad's role is to have fun with his children.

- All dads should be the household disciplinarians.

- It is important for a dad's self-esteem that he is a bread-winner.

- Mums are always more caring than dads.

- Dads are better than mums at teaching DIY and car main-tenance.

- All dads should teach their children sports; men are more competitive than women.

- What unique things can you give to the children in your family?

*

Week 1 assignment

One of the goals of the Daddy Cool! programme is for you to produce a Daddy Cool! scrapbook, which can form part of the legacy you leave for your children. Each week, you will be given an assignment to fill in part of the scrapbook. During the following session you will then get the opportunity to tell the rest of the group about what you have put in your scrapbook and why (but only if you want to do that). If you have more than one child you can choose whether to produce one scrapbook to be shared amongst all your children or a scrapbook for each child.

This week's assignment is to include in the scrapbook:

1. Something to represent you and your child together. This may be a photo, drawing, poem or something else. Be as creative as you like!

2. Your thoughts about what unique things you can give to your child. If you are able to, discuss this with the mother of your children before recording your thoughts. She may give you a different perspective and it will help you to talk together about the different roles you play in bringing up your children. Again, be as creative as you like in the way you represent your thoughts in the scrapbook. For example, you may choose to:

   * write about what you give to your children.
   * include photographs, such as you in your workplace (to represent you as a breadwinner) or you play-wrestling with your child (to represent you as a strengthener).

* draw a picture or symbols to represent you teaching your child a sport or a craft.
* copy an extract from a book about what a father can give to a child.

3. A record of the types of legacy you feel you would most like to leave for your child. For example, you may choose to:

* list the types of legacy.
* include a photograph of you and your wife/partner (to represent a strong marriage/relationship) or you and your child reading a book (to represent a love of books) or you and your child in church (to represent a strong faith).
* draw a picture, perhaps of the 'legacy brick' construction.
* write a story about the qualities of integrity, honesty and friendship.

*

Tuning in

Discuss the following statements and jot down whether you agree or disagree with them. As you do so, write down any thoughts you have about what it means for a father to tune in to a child.

- Just because a dad is physically present with his children, it doesn't mean he is tuned in to them.

- It doesn't matter how little attention we give to our children. What matters most is for us to be around.

- A father who does not live with his children can still ensure that his children feel his presence.

- You can tell whether a father is tuned in to his child by how much time they spend together.

- A father who is tuned in to his children will naturally buy lots of presents for them.

- You know how important your children are to you by how often you think of them.

- Mixing with other adults is much more satisfying than being focused on the children.

- What does it mean for a father to tune in to his children?

*

What I am tuned in to

You have just compiled a prioritised list of what you are tuned in to—your passions, hobbies, interests and pastimes (other than family and children).

Take it in turns to talk about your lists and their implications, using the following questions as a guide:

- Would you agree that the things you have listed at numbers 1 and 2 are most likely to divert your attention from your children? Do they?
- How do you ensure that the balance between the attention you give to your children and the attention you give to the other things in your life remains healthy?
- In what ways can you include your children in your passions, interests and hobbies?

*

Week 2 assignment

This week's assignment is to include in your Daddy Cool! scrapbook:

1. A copy of the 'What I am tuned in to' list that you completed during the session. You may want to insert your children's names and the names of other significant family members at the top of your list. The Daddy Cool! scrapbook will be a gift to your children, so it would be affirming for them to see that you have recorded them as a priority. It will also be good for your children to see what all your passions, hobbies and interests are.

2. Your thoughts about your child. You may want to do so by completing some or all of the following sentences:

   * You are a priority to me because…
   * Having you as my child has given me…
   * The things I love about you are…
   * The things that sometimes mean I can't give you the attention I would like to give are…
   * I tend to get distracted by…
   * When I can give you attention, I enjoy…
   * You make me smile when…

   Alternatively, be as creative as you like to represent your thoughts in some other way. For example, you may choose to:

   * write a poem about how special your child is to you.

* include photographs to complete some or all of the sentences above. For example, you could include a photo of your child smiling as one of the things you love about him or her.
* draw a picture or symbols to represent the things you love about your child.

3. Some information about the passion, interest or hobby that you enjoy most. Share your enthusiasm with your child by including, for example:

* a paragraph about what you enjoy and why.
* a photograph of you taking part in the activity.
* an example of the thing you are interested in. For example, if you love reading the newspaper, you could order a back copy and include the front page of the newspaper from the day your child was born.

You could also try to get your child involved in the activity you enjoy and record the results. For example, accompany your child to a local cricket match, take a child's bat and ball with you, and play cricket together at the side of the pitch. Or, if you play a musical instrument at church or in a band, find a toy version of the instrument and let your child stand with you and copy you by playing along. Take a photo for your scrapbook or write about the experience.

Memories of my father

Which of the following father-type descriptions most accurately portrays your own father as he was when you were a child? It may be that your father had a mixture of the different father-type characteristics, or you may feel that your father is not covered by any of these descriptions.

Explain to the group:

- what your father was like.
- how you are similar to your father in the way you parent your children.
- how you are different from your father in the way you parent your children.

Father type	Characteristics
Indifferent Dad	Not really that keen on children. Content to leave caring for the children's practical and emotional needs to his wife/partner. Rarely initiates any activity with the children, but will do so reluctantly if instructed by his wife/partner. Spends his spare time pursuing his own interests.

Sidelined Dad	Keen to get involved but his wife/partner does not trust him to look after the children properly. When he does get to look after the children, she leaves detailed instructions of how to do it and complains that he 'does it wrong'. Other women in the family, such as his mother-in-law, are allowed to take a more active role in parenting than he is.
Fully Involved Dad	Relishes being a dad and plays an equal part with the mother in caring for the children. Willingly looks after the children's practical and emotional needs. Work sometimes gets in the way but the children are left in no doubt that their dad wants to be with them.
Not Interested Dad	Only agreed to have children to please his wife/partner. He refuses to get involved in caring for the children. Resents the limiting impact it has on his life and hates talking about children and parenting with other parents.
Nervous Dad	Wants to be a good dad but does not feel very confident about his parenting abilities. Accepts his wife's/partner's authority in caring for the children and always looks to her for guidance. For example, he cannot decide what clothes to dress the children in. He is particularly fearful about looking after the children alone, and when he does he makes sure his wife/partner leaves a contact telephone number.

Controlling Dad	This dad feels he knows best. He never seeks advice and is critical of other people's way of parenting. He will often suggest to his wife/partner that she is not doing things for the children in the right way. He is very reluctant to let anyone else look after the children.
Hunter/Gatherer Dad	This father takes a pride in being able to provide for his family. He sees his main role as keeping a roof over the family's head and putting food on the table, and he does it well. He is often out early and gets home from work late. Most of the caring for the children falls to his wife/partner, but he tries to take them to their activities at the weekends.
Distant Dad	He does not live with his children and has little contact with them. He does not get along with their mother and so avoids seeing her. He is also happy to leave responsibility for the children to her. He regards the children as belonging to a previous phase of his life from which he has now moved on. He seldom remembers or bothers with birthdays. He may occasionally initiate contact but only to appease a rare and short-lived prick of conscience. Each contact is followed by a lengthy period of silence.

*

Time and memories survey

You now have an illustration of how you spend the hours in a typical week. Complete the following survey, and then discuss your responses with the rest of your group.

I am happy with the way I spend the hours in my week.
Agree / Disagree

I need to make some changes to the way I spend my time.
Agree / Disagree

The thing I spend too much time doing is _____

The category I spend too little time on is _____

It's not important how much time I spend with my children; it's only important that the time I spend with them is high quality.
Agree / Disagree

It doesn't matter what I do with my children; it's just important that I am around.
Agree / Disagree

The thing that stops me spending more time with my children is _____

Other people control how I spend my time; I can't do anything about it.
Agree / Disagree

The more time I spend with my children, the more they will remember about me.
Agree / Disagree

Memories can't be manufactured; they just happen.
Agree / Disagree

*

Week 3 assignment

This week's assignment is to include in your Daddy Cool! scrapbook:

1. Your memories of your own father. Record the memories you have of your own father by, for example:

   * Writing your memories down. As well as writing about what your father was like, try to include some specific memories of something your dad did (for example, the time he made a mess of a DIY job and you laughed) or something you did together (for example, your memories of going swimming with your dad every Saturday morning) or a description of the jobs/responsibilities your father had (for example, what he did, who he worked with, or what he wore to work).
   * Including photographs that you feel capture the essence of your father or evoke particular memories.
   * Putting something in the scrapbook that your father has passed on to you, such as a copy of a drawing he made or a copy of his birth certificate.

   If, for any reason, you cannot remember your father, record what you know of him from other people's memories or, if that is not possible, express how you imagine your father would have been or even how you would have liked your father to have been if he had been around.

2. Your thoughts on how you would like to be remembered by your own child. You could head the page: 'The three things I would most like you to remember about me are…'. You could then write, draw or include photographs or other items to show how you would like to be remembered as a father. For example, if you would like to be remembered as a breadwinner, include a photograph of you at work, or if you would like your child to remember you as a fun dad, write about the sort of fun things you do that you hope your son or daughter will remember.

3. Something to show what you most like to do with your children. Again, you could write or draw or include photographs to show what you most enjoy doing with your children.

*

Elements of respect

To help you define what characteristics cause children to respect their fathers, note down the names of three people you respect. Alongside each name, write down the three main characteristics that inspire you to respect him or her.

Name	Characteristics
1.	
2.	
3.	

Discuss what you have written with the person next to you, and agree the three characteristics that you feel are most important in helping to inspire respect.

1. _____

2. _____

3. _____

*

Self-audit of respect

The purpose of this exercise is to give you an opportunity to think through your strengths and weaknesses. It is not intended to make you feel guilty, but just to increase your own awareness of what 'respect-inspiring' characteristics you may or may not have.

Write into the table the list of characteristics that the whole group has suggested, and then score yourself against each one, as shown below.

1 = I am excellent at this. I rarely falter.
2 = I display this characteristic most of the time.
3 = Sometimes I'm good at this; sometimes I'm bad.
4 = Occasionally I manage this, but most of the time I struggle.
5 = I'm really bad at this.

Characteristic	1	2	3	4	5

*

Talking and listening briefs

Talking

Speak to the other person for two minutes about either your work or a hobby (or both). A leader will let you know when one minute has passed, and then again when the two minutes are up.

Listening

The other person will speak to you for two minutes about his work or hobby (or both). Please listen attentively (for example, keeping eye contact, nodding head, making 'mmm' sounds) for the first minute. A leader will let you know when one minute has passed. For the second minute, please do not listen attentively. Stop nodding your head, break eye contact, look away and stop making 'mmm' sounds. The speaker does not know that you are going to do this, so do not be surprised if he seems a bit discouraged. A leader will call time when the second minute has passed, and we will get back together to review the exercise.

*

Week 4 assignment

This week's assignment is to include in your Daddy Cool! scrapbook:

1. A record of whom you respect and why. Record the names of the people you respect and some information about why you respect them. You could do this by, for example:

   * writing down names of people and listing the characteristics that make you respect them.
   * recording the details of specific instances in which these people have inspired your respect, such as the care your friend showed in looking after elderly parents, or the patience your friend had when listening to you talk about some difficulties you faced, or the danger a person put herself in to save someone's life.
   * including photographs of the people you respect.
   * recording yourself on tape or disc, talking about the people you respect, and popping the tape/disc into a pouch in your scrapbook.

2. What characteristics you see in your children that you think will, in time, make them good fathers/mothers/role models for their own children. Think about the characteristics your children have already begun to show—such as a love of having fun or a willingness to share or a good sense of right and wrong—that you think will help them to be good parents. Write about them or include photographs showing them having fun, sharing,

and so on. Alternatively, draw pictures to illustrate their characteristics.

3. Something to show what you like to listen to your children talking about—for example, the books they have read, the television programmes they have watched or the things they have done at school. Write, draw, include photographs, or simply recall a time when you and your child had a really good chat together.

Values and beliefs case studies

Below are case studies of three families. Read through the case studies and, for each one, make a list of what the parents do that you feel is good for passing on values and beliefs, and what is bad. Discuss your answers in your groups.

The Smith family

Mr and Mrs Smith have been married for twelve years and have two children, Michael and Lucy. They are a close, secure family. Michael and Lucy go to a church school (Mr and Mrs Smith think that the standard of discipline is better there) and, because of what they are taught at school, the family often discuss religion at home. Mr and Mrs Smith tell their children that they do not believe in God. However, they do acknowledge the worth of Christian values such as kindness, generosity and truthfulness, and they teach their children that these principles are right. It is the family's tradition to have christenings, so Michael and Lucy were christened in the local parish church where Mr and Mrs Smith were married. Mr Smith runs the local junior cricket team. He is highly competitive and, at times, he shows it by encouraging his players to win at all costs, even if it means breaking a few rules. Mrs Smith spends a lot of time caring for her mother, who is ill. Mr Smith works long hours. As a result, he is rapidly rising through the company ranks and the family is financially well-off.

The Jones/Thomas Family

Mr Jones has lived with Miss Thomas for ten years but they have never got round to getting married. They have a son, Daniel, who is nine years old. They never discuss spiritual beliefs between themselves or with Daniel. However, if they were pushed, they would say that they believe there is a God of some sort. In fact, they prayed hard when Daniel was very ill as a baby and it was touch-and-go as to whether or not he would survive. They have strong political views about how a fair society should be run and, in particular, believe that the poorer members of society should be helped by the rich. They contribute financially to the political party they support and give a considerable amount of money to various charities. Mr Jones works part-time and spends the rest of his time looking after the home and Daniel. Miss Thomas works full-time and spends her spare time campaigning for their political party. She sees little of Daniel, other than during the family holiday they take once a year, and this sometimes causes friction between her and Mr Jones. Daniel gets upset when he hears his mum and dad arguing.

The Williams Family

Mr and Mrs Williams are committed Christians and encourage their teenage sons, Carl and Simon, to be so too. They are active members of a church and make their sons go to the service on a Sunday morning. Carl resents this because he would rather play football with his mates. He is also not allowed to watch football on the television on a Sunday afternoon, because it is important to Mr and Mrs Williams to 'keep the sabbath holy': for them, that involves not watching television. Mr Williams loves football too and understands his son's frustration, so he tries to take him to watch games on Saturdays as often as possible. Mr Williams gets very involved in the games and sometimes loses his temper and swears at the referee. He apologises to his son afterwards. Mr and Mrs Williams are very hospitable and regularly hold dinner parties, which their guests always thoroughly enjoy. Mrs Williams sometimes drinks too much alcohol at these parties and embarrasses her husband. At the beginning of each day, the Williams family pray together. Simon will pray. Carl doesn't, but secretly he likes this family ritual.

*

Week 5 assignment

As with previous assignments, feel free to use any format—
words or pictures—to represent the themes of this assignment. However, as it is being completed during the final
session, a specific structure is suggested below. This week's
assignment is to include in your Daddy Cool! scrapbook:

1. A record of your own values and beliefs. You can do so by
   completing the following sentences:
   The three values that are most important to me are… (some
   suggestions are concern for others, honesty, gratitude,
   loyalty, generosity, openness, commitment, trustworthiness,
   tolerance, self-control, patience, reliability, kindness).
   I believe… [a short statement of your spiritual beliefs].

2. A statement of what values and beliefs you hope your
   children will have, and why. Maybe you would like your
   children to have the same values and beliefs as you, in
   which case say so—or perhaps different ones. You could
   start the statements by using the following words:
   I hope the values and beliefs you have will be…
   I would like you to have these values and beliefs because…

3. A final message to your children. This is an opportunity to
   finish off your scrapbook with a positive message to your
   children. For example, you might want to say that you are
   proud of your children, or you are glad they are alive, or
   you are looking forward to sharing in their lives. A good
   way to start your message is:
   [Insert name of child], I would like you to know…

Also by Mark Chester

Who Let The Dads Out?

Inspiring ideas for churches to engage with dads and their preschool children

Parent and toddler work can strengthen families and transform relationships, yet sometimes men have limited access to the parent and toddler world.

This book tells the story of how Who Let The Dads Out? came into being. It gives a practical guide for setting up and running the monthly sessions, complete with theological background, real-life case studies, helpful hints and tips, and twelve easy craft ideas.

Mark Chester is the founder and chairman of the Who Let The Dads Out? national initiative, which began in 2003. He works full time for Liverpool Football Club as their community family officer, where he has established and developed Tactics 4 Families, a schools programme using the language and principles of football to encourage the skills needed in positive family relationships.

ISBN 978 1 84101 885 0   £6.99
Available from your local Christian bookshop or direct from BRF: visit www.brfonline.org.uk

Enjoyed
this book?

Write a review—we'd love to hear what you think.
Email: reviews@brf.org.uk

Keep up to date—receive details of our new books as they happen.
Sign up for email news and select your interest groups at:
www.brfonline.org.uk/findoutmore/

Follow us on Twitter @brfonline

By post—to receive new title information by post (UK only), complete
the form below and post to: BRF Mailing Lists, 15 The Chambers, Vineyard,
Abingdon, Oxfordshire, OX14 3FE

Your Details
Name _____
Address_____
_____
Town/City _____ Post Code _____
Email_____

Your Interest Groups (*Please tick as appropriate)	
☐ Advent/Lent	☐ Messy Church
☐ Bible Reading & Study	☐ Pastoral
☐ Children's Books	☐ Prayer & Spirituality
☐ Discipleship	☐ Resources for Children's Church
☐ Leadership	☐ Resources for Schools

Support your local bookshop
Ask about their new title information schemes.